OBB JUN 4 1996

W9-ARA-184

R00165 14148

J 909.823 Hil

Hills, Ken.

1930s /

Please Do Not Remove Date Due Slip
From Book Pocket

Palm Beach County
Library System

3650 Summit Boulevard
West Palm Beach, FL 33406

DEMCO

TAKE TEN YEARS

1930s

© Copyright this edition 1992, Steck-Vaughn Company

© Original copyright Ken Hills 1991

All rights reserved. No part of this publication may be reproduced,
stored in a retrieval system, or transmitted, in any form or by any
means, electronic, mechanical, photocopying, recording, or otherwise,
without prior permission of the publisher.

Library of Congress Cataloging-in-Publication Data

Hills, Ken.
   1930s / Ken Hills.
      p. cm. — (Take ten years)
   Includes bibliographical references and index.
   Summary: Explores the decade of the 1930s worldwide, a time which
included the Depression, Gandhi's defiance of British rule in India,
the Spanish Civil War, and the abdication of Edward VIII.
   ISBN 0-8114-3076-6
   1. History, Modern—20th century—Juvenile literature.
[1. History, Modern—20th century.] I. Title. II. Series.
D720.H56 1991   91–42164
909.82′3—dc20   CIP
                                        AC

Typeset by Multifacit Graphics, Keyport, NJ
Printed in Spain by GRAFO, S.A., Bilbao
Bound in the United States by Lake Book, Melrose Park, IL
1 2 3 4 5 6 7 8 9 0 LB 97 96 95 94 93 92

Acknowledgments

Maps — Jillian Luff, Bitmap Graphics
Design — Neil Sayer
Editor — Jean Coppendale

For permission to reproduce copyright material the author and publishers
gratefully acknowledge the following:

Cover photographs — Franklin Delano Roosevelt Library/H.R. Fechner;
UPI/Bettmann Newsphotos; The Hulton Picture Company; Smithsonian
Institution, National Air & Space Museum

Pages 4 and 5 — Popperfoto, The Vintage Magazine Co., The Hulton
Picture Company; Topham; page 8 — Popperfoto; page 9 — (top) The
Hulton Picture Company, (bottom) Topham; page 10 — (top) The
Illustrated London News Picture Library, (bottom) Topham; page 11 —
(left) UPI/Bettmann, (top) Popperfoto, (bottom) Topham; page 12 — (left)
H. Armstrong Roberts, (right) The Bettmann Archive; page 13 —
UPI/Bettmann; page 14 — (left) The Illustrated London News Picture
Library, (top, bottom left, bottom right) The Vintage Magazine Co.; page
15 — (left) The Hulton Picture Company, (right) The Illustrated London
News Picture Library; page 16 — The Illustrated London News Picture
Library; page 17 — The Vintage Magazine Co.; page 18 — The Hulton
Picture Company; page 19 — The Hulton Picture Company; page 20 —
(top, bottom) The Illustrated London News Picture Library, (middle) The
Vintage Magazine Co.; page 21 — (left) The Hulton Picture Company,
(right) Topham; page 22 — (left top) The Hulton Picture Company, (left
bottom) UPI/Bettmann Newsphotos, (right) Topham; page 23 — (left)
Barnaby's Picture Library, (middle, top right) The Hulton Picture
Company/The Bettmann Archive, (bottom right) The Illustrated London
News Picture Library; page 24 — Topham; page 26 — (top) The Hulton
Picture Company/The Bettmann Archive, (bottom) Topham; page 27 —
(left) Topham, (right) UPI/Bettmann Newsphotos; page 28 — The
Illustrated London News Picture Library; page 29 — (left) Topham, (top)
The Vintage Magazine Co., (right) UPI/Bettmann; page 31 — (left, top
right) Topham, (right center) UPI/Bettmann; page 32 — (top) Topham,
(middle) The Hulton Picture Company/The Bettmann Archive, (bottom)
Associated Press/Topham; page 33 — (left) Topham, (top right) Barnaby's
Picture Library, (bottom right) The Illustrated London News Picture
Library; page 34 — Topham; page 36 — (top left) Colorsport, (bottom
left) UPI/Bettmann Newsphotos, (top right) The Vintage Magazine Co.;
page 37 — (left) The Hulton Picture Company, (right) Topham; page 38
— UPI/Bettmann Newsphotos; page 40 — UPI/Bettmann; page 41 —
(top) Topham, (bottom) The Vintage Magazine Co.; page 42 — (left) The
Vintage Magazine Co., (right) Topham; page 43 — (left) Franklin D.
Roosevelt Library, (right) The Hulton Picture Company; pages 44 and 45
— The Vintage Magazine Co., Topham, Bill Sharman/Colin Garratt's
Steam Locomotives of the World Photo Library.

TAKE TEN YEARS

1930s

KEN HILLS

PALM BEACH COUNTY
LIBRARY SYSTEM
3650 Summit Boulevard
West Palm Beach, FL 33406-4198

RAINTREE
STECK-VAUGHN
L I B R A R Y

Austin, Texas

Contents

4

The pictures on page 4 show
Lines of unemployed women, northern England
Lines of unemployed, New York City
Al Capone facing charges of not paying taxes
President Franklin D. Roosevelt
Brownshirted Nazis marching at a Nuremberg rally
Rolls Royce Phantom II
Adolf Hitler

The pictures on page 5 show
Poster advertising 1936 Olympic Games in Berlin
Cover of British *Coronation Song Book*, 1937
Cover of *Mickey Mouse Annual*
Newspaper seller on the day Britain declared war,
   September 3, 1939

Introduction

World War I ended just over ten years before the thirties began. It had been the most destructive war in history, and it left large parts of Europe in ruins. Slowly during the twenties even those countries that had lost most in the War started to recover. All over the world, living conditions began to improve.

America in the twenties seemed to be entering a golden age. New industries appeared, such as the production of cars and motion pictures, and radio programs developed. Many people grew rich and the American public could afford to spend at a record rate. It looked as though the good times would go on forever.

As the thirties began, the good times became hard times. America's boom collapsed. The Great Depression, as it was called, spread from America around the world. Businesses were ruined, and millions of workers lost their jobs. They and their families faced a future without hope.

In their misery, the unemployed rebelled. They joined in protest marches. They rioted, and fought the police who tried to stop them. It seemed that law and order was crumbling in many countries.

The crisis made governments everywhere reshape their policies. In the United States, President Roosevelt's New Deal policy gradually led the country back towards prosperity and in Europe as well, little by little, the nations recovered.

In Germany, Adolf Hitler promised the people simple solutions to their problems. He offered them strong leadership, and armed Germany for war. On the other side of the world, Japan set out to conquer her giant neighbor China. Other nations were too timid or too busy with their own problems to face these threats to world peace. As the thirties ended, countries that had tried to keep the peace prepared most urgently for war. War came, in Europe, in September 1939.

YEARS	WORLD AFFAIRS
1930	Worldwide depression. Tragedy of peasants in Russia. In India, Gandhi defies the British.
1931	Japanese troops drive Chinese from Manchuria. Japan's expansion policy goes into effect.
1932	Roosevelt's election cheers America. British jail Gandhi in India. Nazi support grows in Germany
1933	Nazis win power in Germany. Reichstag burns down. Spain in turmoil.
1934	Nazis murder Austrian Chancellor. Hitler does away with his rivals.
1935	Hitler scraps the Versailles Treaty. League of Nations bans sale of arms to Italy.
1936	Roosevelt re-elected U.S. President. German troops enter the Rhineland. Europe's protests ignored.
1937	Chamberlain becomes British Prime Minister. Japan bombs U.S. ship and apologizes.
1938	Germany seizes Austria and threatens Czechoslovakia. A meeting in Munich prevents war.
1939	Germany swallows the rest of Czechoslovakia and threatens Poland. Europe prepares for war.

WARS	PEOPLE	EVENTS
	American Sinclair Lewis wins Nobel Prize for literature. Abyssinia's new emperor, Haile Selassie, crowned.	German Nazis attack Jews. Giant airship *R101* crashes. New planet Pluto discovered.
Japan and China fight in Manchuria.	Inventor Thomas Edison dies. Campbell sets new landspeed record. Scarface Al Capone jailed.	George Washington Bridge opens in New York. Huge earthquake in New Zealand. World's tallest building opens in New York.
Fighting in Manchuria spreads to China. Japanese officers kill their prime minister.	Lindbergh baby kidnapped. George Eastman, inventor of Kodak camera, dies. Amelia Earhart sets Atlantic record.	Los Angeles Olympic Games. Dutch win land from the sea. Sydney's new bridge opened.
	F.D. Roosevelt becomes President. Campbell sets new landspeed record. Writer H.G. Wells predicts world war in seven years.	Japan and Germany quit League of Nations. Prohibition ends in America. First around-the-world solo flight.
Civil war in China. Nationalists surround Communist Red Army. Border fighting in Abyssinia.	Composer Sir Edward Elgar dies. Death of Marie Curie. German children join movement supporting Hitler.	Quintuplets born in Canada. Huge earthquake in India. Women in shorts at Wimbledon Tennis Championships.
In China the Red Army fights its way to safety. Italians invade Abyssinia.	President Roosevelt signs Social Security Act. George Gershwin's brilliant new opera.	Nazis ban jazz music. Americans set new altitude record. Dust storms destroy U.S. farms.
Civil war breaks out in Spain. European powers agree to keep out. Germany occupies the Rhineland.	Britain's king Edward VIII gives up the throne. American playwright Eugene O'Neill wins Nobel Prize for literature.	Jesse Owens triumphs at Berlin Olympics. Record Atlantic crossing by airship *Hindenburg*. Prince Farouk becomes king of Egypt.
Civil war rages in Spain. German aircraft destroy Guernica. Japanese advance in China.	President Franklin D. Roosevelt inaugurated for second term. Joe Louis becomes world heavyweight boxing champion. Composer George Gershwin dies.	German airship *Hindenburg* explodes. Plan for division of Palestine proposed.
War in Spain goes on. Franco is winning.	Roosevelt signs Fair Labor Standards Act. Disney cartoon success.	Italy wins World Cup at soccer. Night of terror for Germany's Jews.
Franco's victory in Spain's civil war. Germany invades Poland. World War II begins.	Entertainer Judy Garland stars in *Wizard of Oz*.	World's Fair opens in New York. America's first television program. First passengers fly the Atlantic.

1930

WORLD SLUMP

WORLD TRADE IN DANGER

June, Washington President Hoover is increasing taxes on all imported goods. He intends to make foreign goods so expensive that Americans will buy things made in America instead. In reply some countries are threatening to increase taxes on American imports. If many countries do this, no country will be able to sell goods to another and world trade will be strangled.

MILLIONS OUT OF WORK IN U.S.A.

Oct., Washington Three million people are out of work in the United States. Their numbers are rising rapidly. Thousands of businesses are closing down. Over 60,000 workers are losing their jobs every week.

Lines of unemployed people in New York City waiting for free food.

BRITAIN'S ECONOMIC PROBLEMS

Oct., London One and a half million workers in Britain have lost their jobs. The numbers of those out of work grow week by week. Businesses are closing down. No end to the crisis is in sight.

A demonstration by unemployed people in London.

Police and jobless workers clash in London

Oct. 15, London Fighting broke out in the East End of London this afternoon. The scuffles began when police tried to stop out-of-work men marching through the streets to protest about the lack of jobs. The police are preparing for more trouble as the number of those without jobs increases.

AMERICA'S ECONOMIC CRISIS

Dec. 11, Washington America's economic problems are getting worse. A major bank, the Bank of the United States, has collapsed. Half a million people kept their savings there. Now it has no money to pay them and they have lost everything.

ECONOMIC CRISIS IS WORLDWIDE

Dec., It has been estimated that 30 million people are without work in the industrial countries of the world. No nation has escaped the crisis. The situation in Germany is particularly bad. Nearly half of all men between 16 and 30 are without jobs.

A sign of the economic depression in Germany. In Berlin, hundreds of cars are stored in a garage in order to avoid heavy taxation.

GANDHI DEFIES BRITISH LAWS

May 4, Dandi, India The British authorities have arrested Mahatma Gandhi. His crime was picking up and eating a piece of salt! In India, salt is taxed and only the government is allowed to make it and sell it. Gandhi came to Dandi on foot with a few followers. He walked down to the sea, picked up some dried salt from the sand, and ate it. By doing that, he broke the law. Thousands of Indians have now done the same. The British cannot arrest them all, so they have arrested Gandhi.

The Mahatma plans to go on breaking British laws, but never to use violence. Millions of Indians obey Gandhi and if they follow his example, British rule is bound to break down and India will win independence.

Gandhi (marked by arrow) and some followers defying the law by picking up salt.

Nazis triumph in German elections

Sept. 15, Berlin The National Socialist party has won 107 seats in the German parliament. It is now the second largest party in Germany behind the Socialists. The National Socialists have shortened their name to "Nazi." Their leader is Herr Adolf Hitler. Some people say that he will become chancellor of Germany before long.

THE TERRIBLE PENALTY OF BEING RICH IN RUSSIA

March, Moscow The richer peasants in Russia have suffered a terrible fate in the recent changes. These peasants, or "kulaks" as they are called, have not been allowed to join the new collective farms. On Stalin's orders, the men are sent to concentration camps. The women and children have been packed off to Siberia, without proper food or shelter. As a result about a million families have been condemned to die from overwork, cold, or starvation.

Russian peasants recovering hidden grain that would otherwise be taken by the government.

Millions of Russian peasants forced to move

Feb., Moscow The Soviet government claims that half the peasants in Russia have joined collective farms. Russia is a huge country. Most of its people work on the land. The government statement means that no fewer than 60 million people have been forced to move from their homes inside two months. These changes have been forced on the Russian people by their leader, Joseph Stalin.

NEWS IN BRIEF . . .

NEW PLANET DISCOVERED

March 18, Arizona An astronomer working at the Lovell Observatory has discovered a new planet going around the sun. He has called it Pluto, after the Greek god of the underworld.

NOBEL PRIZE GOES TO SINCLAIR LEWIS

Dec. 12, Stockholm, Sweden Sinclair Lewis today accepted the Nobel Prize for literature. Lewis is the first American writer to win this honor. He has been a famous novelist since 1920. Lewis uses satire to criticize the standards and values of the middle class in machine-age America.

In his acceptance speech here, Lewis named several other noted American authors he considered equally deserving of the prize. Among them were Ernest Hemingway, Willa Cather, and Sherwood Anderson.

In 1926, Sinclair Lewis refused to accept the Pulitzer Prize for his novel *Arrowsmith*, an attack on the medical profession.

Lewis and his wife, noted columnist Dorothy Thompson.

The skeleton of the *R101* airship which crashed on its maiden flight.

THE WORLD'S LARGEST AIRSHIP IS DESTROYED

Oct. 5, Beauvais, France The British airship *R101* crashed here early this morning and burst into flames. It flew into a hillside and exploded. Only 8 people survived of the 54 on board.

NAZIS ATTACK JEWS IN GERMANY

Oct. 15, Berlin The Nazi leader Herr Adolf Hitler has made many threats against the Jews. His followers are now carrying them out. Crowds of Nazi supporters have paraded through the streets of Berlin shouting, "Death to the Jews!" Nazi party members dressed in their brownshirt uniforms have broken Jewish shop windows and smashed up what is inside. There are reports that the Nazis have also attacked Jews in other parts of Germany.

HAILE SELASSIE CROWNED EMPEROR OF ABYSSINIA

Nov. 2, Addis Ababa, Abyssinia Thousands of warriors dressed in lionskin cloaks have come to Addis Ababa to see their emperor crowned. There are only two black rulers in the whole of Africa. Emperor Haile Selassie is one. The president of Liberia is the other.

1931

"Star-Spangled Banner" is Official Anthem

March 3, Washington President Hoover today received a bill from Congress naming "The Star-Spangled Banner" as our national anthem. The famous words were written by Francis Scott Key in 1814. It has served as the unofficial anthem of the United States for 100 years and has been played by military bands since the 1890s. Now this rousing song is legally the national anthem.

GHANDI VISITS KING OF ENGLAND

Nov. 4, London Mahatma Ghandi is shown being interviewed by reporters in front of 10 Downing St., home of Britain's Prime Minister. Ghandi is India's greatest leader in its struggle for independence from Britain. He has been in and out of British jails since 1922. However, today he was among the 500 guests of King George and Queen Mary at a party in Buckingham Palace.

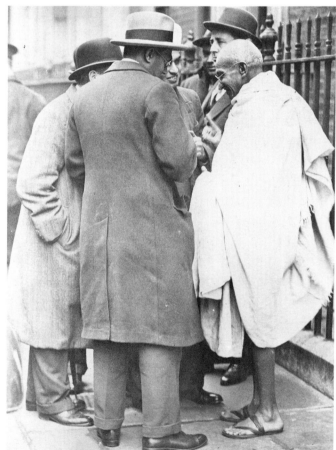

Serious outbreak of fighting in Manchuria

Sept. 19, Manchuria, Northern China Fighting has broken out between Japanese and Chinese troops in this northeastern area of Asia. The Japanese have already captured the Chinese city of Mukden. They blame China for starting the trouble. The Japanese authorities say that they drove Chinese troops out of Mukden to stop them blowing up the railroad line that runs through the city. The Chinese strongly deny this accusation.

The Japanese hold southern Manchuria on lease from China. They have factories and mines in the area, and they own the railroad. Troops from Japan are stationed there to protect Japan's interests. The fighting continues.

Japan's economy has been badly hit by the current depression. The attack on Mukden, in Manchuria, is seen as the first step in a policy of expansion into China which would provide a vast additional international market for Japanese goods.

Manchurian conquest strengthens war party in Japan

Dec. 30, Tokyo, Japan Japanese troops have driven the Chinese from Manchuria. A warlike spirit has seized Japan and it is not safe to speak out against it. The government is despised for giving in to the League of Nations. Power is falling into the hands of those who wish Japan to conquer an empire.

SPAIN BECOMES A REPUBLIC

April 14, Madrid, Spain The socialists have won the elections. King Alfonso has gone into exile and Spain will now become a republic. Church and army leaders are bitterly opposed to this prospect. They fear a republic would be the first step towards communism. They would fight to prevent it.

GEORGE WASHINGTON BRIDGE OPENS TODAY

Oct. 24, New York City A crowd gathered today for the opening ceremonies of the George Washington Bridge. A major architectural and engineering feat, the 4,800-foot-long bridge spans the Hudson River. It links New York City and New Jersey.

NEWS IN BRIEF . . .

HUGE EARTHQUAKE IN NEW ZEALAND

Feb. 3, New Zealand A violent earthquake has almost destroyed the towns of Napier and Hastings in New Zealand's North Island. Over two hundred people died as their houses collapsed upon them — 950 have been injured and 10,000 are homeless.

MALCOLM CAMPBELL SETS NEW RECORD

Feb. 5, Daytona Beach, Florida Captain Campbell today raised his own world landspeed record. In his streamlined *Blue Bird* motorcar, he set a new record of 245 mph.

Captain Campbell in his *Blue Bird*. The car is designed with an unusual tail plane, suggesting an airplane body on wheels.

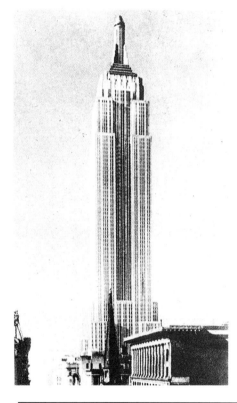

The Empire State Building which was opened by President Hoover in New York.

THE WORLD'S TALLEST BUILDING OPENED

May 1, New York President Hoover has opened the world's tallest building here in New York on Fifth Avenue. He named it the Empire State Building. It has 102 floors and is 1,238 feet high. It contains 10,000,000 bricks, and there is an airship mooring-mast at the top. Construction began on March 17, 1930 and it cost about $41 million to build.

A NATION OF FILM-GOERS

Sept., London The movies have become the most popular form of entertainment in Britain. A recent survey reveals that over 40 percent of British people see a movie at least once every week.

"SCARFACE" AL CAPONE GOES TO JAIL

Oct. 22 "Scarface" Al Capone, the gangster who made millions from selling illegal alcohol, has been jailed for 11 years. No one was brave enough to give evidence against Capone. The FBI got him in the end for not paying his taxes!

DEATH OF THOMAS EDISON

Oct. 18, New Jersey Thomas Alva Edison died here today aged 84. Edison made over a thousand inventions. He invented the electric light bulb, the phonograph (or gramophone), and many of the devices that make movies possible. Edison will be buried on October 21st. Lights across America will be dimmed for one minute that day, in his honor.

1932

CHINESE GOVERNMENT BANS JAPANESE GOODS

Jan. 4, Nanking, China The Chinese government has placed a ban on all imports from Japan. Officials say the ban will stay until the Japanese end the fighting in Manchuria. The ban will hurt the Japanese badly. They depend on the huge Chinese market for the sale of their goods.

WAR SPREADS TO CHINA

Feb. 4, Shanghai, China The ban on Japanese goods has not stopped the war in Manchuria. The fighting has now spread to China itself. A few days ago, the Japanese army in Manchuria launched a successful attack on Shanghai, China's greatest port. The Japanese claim they have seized Shanghai to punish the Chinese for banning their goods.

MANCHURIA BECOMES MANCHUKUO

Feb. 19, Manchukuo Japan now controls Manchuria, and has renamed the country Manchukuo. The Japanese claim that Manchukuo is a free and independent state. In fact, the new government takes its orders from the Japanese authorities in Tokyo. The truth is that Manchukuo is now part of the Japanese empire.

JAPAN'S PRIME MINISTER KILLED

March 16, Tokyo Prime Minister Inukai of Japan has been murdered. Last night, a group of young officers entered his house and shot him dead. Inukai angered the army when he tried to end the war in Manchuria. This is why he was killed. His murderers belong to the "League of Blood," a secret society of officers that aims to make Japan great by conquering an empire. Japan is now in their hands. The prospects for peace are bleak.

One of the Chinese trenches in Shanghai.

Prime Minister Inukai of Japan.

America elects new President

Nov. 8, Washington Americans have elected a new leader. Out goes President Hoover. In comes Franklin D. Roosevelt.

Mr. Roosevelt is 50 years old, and has been a successful and popular governor of New York State. He is paralyzed from the waist down by polio but his handicap has not reduced his energy, or his cheerfulness. The hopes of America will be with this young politician when he takes over as President next year.

Franklin D. Roosevelt is seen here as a presidential candidate campaigning for votes in Pittsburgh. The main issue in the election was the trade depression and unemployment.

BRITISH ARREST GANDHI

Jan. 6, Delhi, India Two days ago, Mahatma Gandhi was arrested by the British authorities. Today other leading members of the Indian National Congress party are being rounded up and imprisoned.

The British, who rule India, have promised that one day India will have self-government. Gandhi and his followers want independence now. Their Congress party has been declared illegal.

Herr Hitler loses the election, but claims a victory

April 10, Berlin Field Marshal von Hindenburg remains president of Germany. In the election he beat Adolf Hitler, leader of the Nazi party, by six million votes.

Although Herr Hitler did not win the election, he easily came in second. The Nazis received over three times more votes than did their chief opponents, the Communists. Herr Hitler claims this as a great victory.

LINDBERGH BABY KIDNAPPED

March 2, N.J. The biggest manhunt in the history of this nation is under way for the kidnapper of the infant son of Charles A. Lindbergh, famous transatlantic flyer. Among the clues in last night's crime are footprints, a ladder, and a note. The contents of the note have not been disclosed.

HUNGER MARCHERS IN LONDON

Oct. 27, "The workers kept the police back from the meetings; several times mounted police charged forward, only to be repulsed by thousands of workers who tore up railings and used them as weapons and barricades for the protection of their meetings. Many mounted men were dragged from their horses. From the streets the fighting extended into the park and back again into the streets, where repeated mounted police charges at full speed failed to dislodge the workers. The foot police were on several occasions surrounded by strong forces of workers, and terrific fights ensued."

(Wal Hannington, *Unemployed Struggles* 1919–36)

NEWS IN BRIEF . . .

MAN WHO MADE PHOTOGRAPHY EASY DIES

March 14, Rochester, N.Y. George Eastman made taking photographs easy and inexpensive. Over 50 years ago he invented roll film, and a camera to use it in. He called his camera a "Kodak." He thought up this phrase to sell it: "You press the button, we do the rest." The Kodak sold in millions, and George Eastman became a very rich man. He was generous, too. In 1930, he gave away half a million of his cameras to the children of this country. George Eastman died today. He was 77.

George Eastman pictured with his Kodak camera.

SYDNEY'S NEW BRIDGE

May 19, Sydney, Australia The new bridge over Sydney's magnificent harbor was opened today. It is 1,560 ft. long and 148 ft. wide, and is the largest bridge of its kind in the world. It carries eight lanes for cars, a bicycle lane, two railroad tracks as well as sidewalks for people on foot.

AMERICA'S AMELIA EARHART SETS ATLANTIC RECORD

May 21, Dublin, Ireland Amelia Earhart is the first woman to fly the Atlantic alone. She also made the journey in record time. Her solo flight from Newfoundland to western Ireland took 15 hours and 18 minutes.

THE LOS ANGELES OLYMPIC GAMES

Aug. 14, Los Angeles The U.S.A. has won more medals than any other country at the Los Angeles Games. Few competitors came from Europe. The trip by ship and train costs too much and takes too long. For the first time in any Games, the men athletes lived in an "Olympic Village" built specially for the occasion. The women stayed in hotels. There were other "firsts" in these Games. Electrical devices timed the track events and the races were filmed.

WINNING LAND FROM THE SEA IN HOLLAND

Aug., The Hague, Holland Dutch engineers are building walls around shallow stretches of sea along the Dutch coast. When the wall is finished, the water inside is pumped out. After the seabed has dried out it becomes rich farmland. The engineers have finished a wall 20 mi. long around part of the Zuider Zee. The Dutch say their drainage plans will make Holland 6 percent larger than it is today.

A FRIGHTENING VIEW OF THE FUTURE

Sept., London The most talked-about novel of the year is Aldous Huxley's *Brave New World*. The story is set in Britain many years in the future. Babies are mass-produced in test tubes. Drugs keep the people contented and obedient. Not all the things Mr. Huxley writes about are really impossible. Some of them could happen now!

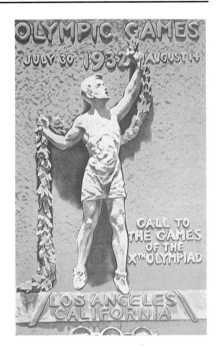

1933

GERMANY'S NEW LEADER

ADOLF HITLER TO LEAD GERMANY

Jan. 30, Berlin President von Hindenburg has appointed the Nazi leader Adolf Hitler Chancellor of Germany. Herr Hitler names Jews and Communists Germany's chief enemies and has boasted that he will destroy them. Now that he has the power, many fear he will do so.

The first picture of Herr Adolf Hitler (center) and his ministers after his appointment as Chancellor of Germany.

FIRE WRECKS REICHSTAG

Feb. 28, Berlin Last night the Reichstag building in Berlin, home of Germany's parliament, was set alight. The fire was watched by Germany's new Chancellor, Herr Hitler, who had hurried to the scene. A young Dutchman, said to have been found in the building, has been held for questioning by the police. He is believed to be a Communist.

As a result German police across the country are rounding up leading Communists and others known to oppose the Nazi party.

HITLER ACCUSES THE COMMUNISTS

March 1, Berlin Chancellor Hitler has just issued a proclamation blaming the Communists for the Reichstag fire. He warns the German people that the blaze was actually meant as a signal for a Communist revolution to break out. Swift action by the police, acting on his orders, put the criminals behind bars, he claims.

Hitler voted dictator of Germany

March 23, Berlin Nazi members cheered wildly as Germany's parliament gave Chancellor Hitler the power to make his own laws. The vote was a farce, for nearly all members of parliament who would have voted against Hitler have been arrested, or are in hiding. But under the new act, Hitler becomes legally, the absolute, unchallenged ruler of Germany.

THE REICHSTAG FIRE

Feb. 27, Berlin "The fire broke out at 9:45 tonight in the Assembly Hall of the Reichstag... Five minutes after the fire had broken out I was outside the Reichstag watching the flames licking their way up the great dome into the tower.

After about twenty minutes of fascinated watching I suddenly saw the famous black motor car of Adolf Hitler slide past, followed by another car containing his personal bodyguard. I rushed after them and was just in time to attach myself to the fringe of Hitler's party as they entered the Reichstag.

We strode across a lobby filled with smoke. The police barred the way. 'The candelabra may crash any moment, Herr Chancellor,' said a captain of the police, with his arms outstretched. By a detour we next reached a part of the building which was actually in flames. Firemen were pouring water into the red mass. Hitler watched them for a few moments, a savage fury blazing from his pale blue eyes...

It was then that Hitler turned to me. 'God grant,' he said, 'that this is the work of the Communists. You are witnessing the beginning of a great new epoch in German history. This fire is the beginning.'"

(D. Sefton Delmer,
Daily Express, Feb. 28, 1933)

The ruins of the Reichstag.

Spain in turmoil

Jan. 20, Madrid Disorder is spreading throughout Spain. Rival right and left wing groups of peasants and workers are in violent conflict. Parliament has given Prime Minister Azaña power to use troops to keep order, but parts of the country are already controlled by the military. Spain seems to be heading for civil war.

CONCENTRATION CAMPS

March 20, Berlin Germany's Nazi government is determined to crush all resistance. Establishments called "concentration camps" are planned as places where those who oppose Nazi rule will be held for what is termed "re-education and training." The first of these camps has opened at Dachau near Munich. The job of running it has been given to Munich's police chief, Heinrich Himmler.

WALKOUTS WEAKEN THE LEAGUE

Oct. 14, Geneva, Switzerland Germany has joined Japan and walked out of the League of Nations. In Berlin, Herr Hitler blames unjust and insulting treatment of his country for the withdrawal.

These walkouts have seriously weakened the League's authority. Few now believe that it has the power to keep the world at peace.

New President's words of hope

March 4, Washington Franklin Delano Roosevelt has been sworn in as President of the United States. In his election address he promised a "New Deal" for America. Now in a stirring first speech as President, he has outlined 100 days of action to set America on the road to recovery. "The only thing we have to fear, is fear itself," is his brave message to the American people.

NEWS IN BRIEF . . .

"WAR IN 7 YEARS" SAYS H. G. WELLS

A second world war breaking out in 1940 is the frightening theme of H. G. Wells' latest scientific romance *The Shape of Things to Come*. This story of the future describes the world in ruins after nine years of world conflict. But a world government is set up after the war, and all the people of the Earth live happily together in peace and justice.

THE LATEST FASHIONS FOR WOMEN!

THE WORLD'S FINEST CAR

Latest in the line of superb motor cars produced by the Rolls-Royce company is the 40–50 hp Phantom II. With a continental body and weighing 2½ tons, it can reach a top speed of over 90 mph. Fuel consumption ranges from 10 mpg in town, to 14 mpg on the open road. Price, with a continental touring body, is about $9,700.

BAD TABLE MANNERS WIN OSCAR!

In the banquet scene from the British film *The Private Life of Henry VIII*, the beefy monarch rips meat with his bare fingers, and tosses half-eaten legs of chicken over his shoulder! British actor Charles Laughton plays the king and clearly enjoys this display of bad table manners. Charles Laughton's performance has won him an Oscar as movies' best actor for 1933.

NEW LANDSPEED RECORD

March 22, Driving his *Blue Bird* motor car at Daytona Beach, Florida, Britain's Sir Malcolm Campbell has set a new world landspeed record at 272 mph.

FIRST SOLO FLIGHT AROUND THE WORLD

May 22, American pilot Wiley Post has become the first person to make a solo flight around the world. Flying a Lockheed Vega aircraft called *Winnie Mae*, the journey took 7 days, 18 hours, 49 minutes.

ALCOHOLIC DRINK ON SALE AGAIN

Dec. 31, On December 5 the law banning alcoholic drink in the United States was ended. Soon it will be possible to buy alcohol, legally, anywhere in the country.

The ban was called "Prohibition." It led to war between rival criminal gangs who fought over the huge fortunes made from selling illegal liquor.

1934

LEADING NAZIS KILLED

June 30, Munich The leading Nazi Ernst Roehm has been murdered. Several of his closest friends died with him. They were staying at a luxury hotel near Munich. There are strong rumors that hundreds of other members of the Nazi party have been killed elsewhere in Germany.

DOUBTS CAST ON HITLER'S STORY

July 26, Vienna More information has been given about the murder of the Austrian Chancellor. After the Nazi gunmen were surrounded they tried to bargain for a safe passage to the German border. If they knew that they would be safe in Germany, it casts doubt on Hitler's word that Germany had nothing to do with the crime.

Adolf Hitler at a Nazi party rally with some supporters. It is believed that Hitler himself ordered the murder of hundreds of his own Nazi Storm Troopers. This group had helped Hitler in his rise to power by disposing of his opponents.

THE AUSTRIAN CHANCELLOR MURDERED

July 25, Vienna, Austria At noon today, armed men entered the offices of Herr Dollfuss, Chancellor of Austria. They made straight for the Chancellor and shot him at point-blank range. Police and troops swiftly surrounded the building, but they were unable to save Herr Dollfuss. The gunmen would not let a doctor in to see him, and he bled to death. It has been revealed that Herr Dollfuss was shot by members of the Austrian Nazi party. They are to be put on trial for murder.

Herr Hitler spoke about the tragic events earlier today in Vienna. He said there are no links between the German Nazi party and the Austrian Nazis who shot Herr Dollfuss.

Austrian Chancellor Dr. Dollfuss lies in state guarded by soldiers of the federal army.

THE STRUGGLE FOR CHINA

March, Kiangsi Province, China The Communists occupy part of Kiangsi Province in southern China. They are led by a man who was once a peasant. His name is Mao Tse-Tung. He calls his followers "The Red Army." Mao and the Communists are fighting General Chiang Kai-Shek and his Nationalist army for the control of China.

Mao's Red Army is in great danger. General Chiang Kai-Shek's forces have surrounded it with a ring of concrete blockhouses and barbed-wire fences. General Chiang intends to starve the Red Army into surrender by cutting off its supplies.

Quintuplets Born

May 28, Ontario, Canada Five girls were born today to Elzire and Oliva Dionne. Their names are Emilie, Marie, Cecile, Yvonne, and Annette.

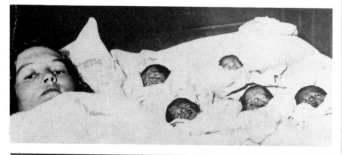

Italy in border shooting

Dec. 18, Abyssinian border Shots have been fired across the border between Abyssinian and Italian troops in East Africa. Each side blames the other for firing first. Italian planes have since bombed two Abyssinian villages near the frontier.

THE RED ARMY BREAKS OUT

Oct., Kiangsi Province The Red Army is on the move. It has broken through Chiang Kai-Shek's troops and is travelling westward toward Kweichow. Mao is keeping away from towns and cities, and is leading his troops through areas where there are very few people. The Nationalists are attacking them along the way, but so far have failed to stop the march of Mao's men.

HITLER THE SPEECH-MAKER

Herr Hitler prepares his speeches as carefully as an actor preparing for a play. First, he makes a recording of what he is going to say. Then he listens to it, over and over again, and practices the gestures and the movements he will use when he delivers the speech to an audience. Huge crowds are hypnotized by his performance. The power of his speech-making helps to explain why the German people are so willing to follow him.

Hitler has promised to build a prosperous new Germany, where the people would have jobs and new pride in their country. He is known for his emotional and often violent speeches made before vast numbers of supporters at Nazi party rallies.

NEWS IN BRIEF . . .

GERMAN CHILDREN READY TO DIE FOR HITLER

Germany When they are ten, boys in Germany have to join the Young People's Movement. They wear miniature Nazi uniforms and are drilled like soldiers. When they join the movement they go through a special ceremony. They stand under a Nazi flag and say this:

"Under this flag, I swear to give all my strength to Adolf Hitler, the man who saved our country. I am willing and ready to die for him, so help me God."

COMPOSER EDWARD ELGAR DIES

Feb. 23, Worcester, England Sir Edward Elgar died today, aged 76. His symphonies, concertos, and choral works have become famous worldwide. He is perhaps best known for composing *Land of Hope and Glory*, which is sometimes called England's second national anthem.

THE GERMAN GREETING

Germany People in Germany are greeting one another in a new way. When two people meet, they thrust out their right arms straight toward each other and say "Heil Hitler!"

The Nazi government has ordered all Germans to use this form of greeting in the future.

SHORTS AT WIMBLEDON

May, London Women competitors are to be allowed to wear shorts instead of skirts at this year's Wimbledon tennis championships. The decision has upset many male officials. They argue that those who play at Wimbledon should set an example of how to dress properly. They say that shorts are vulgar and unfeminine for women.

DEATH OF MARIE CURIE

July 4, France Marie Curie, the world's greatest woman scientist, has died at 66. Madame Curie was born in Poland, but came to France to study science. She married the French scientist Pierre Curie, and in 1903 they were jointly awarded a Nobel Prize for their discovery of radium and radioactivity. Marie Curie died of a blood disease caused by working with radioactive materials.

DILLINGER DEAD

July 22, Chicago John Dillinger, bank robber and murderer of 16 people, lies dead this evening outside a Chicago movie theater. The police were taking no chances with the man who has outwitted them several times. Dillinger fell under a storm of bullets as he came out into the street. He had been watching a gangster movie!

NEW OCEAN LINER LAUNCHED

Sept. 26, Glasgow, Scotland The first ship in history to weigh over 75,000 tons was launched at the John Brown shipyards today. The monster ocean liner will join the Cunard White Star fleet on the Atlantic run, between Southampton, England and New York City. It is expected to go into service in 1936. The new ship's name will be *Queen Mary*.

1935

HITLER TEARS UP THE VERSAILLES TREATY

March 16, Berlin Hitler has scrapped the treaty that ended World War I. The treaty limited the size of Germany's army and navy, and banned it from having an air force. Hitler's move enables him to build up Germany's armed forces exactly as he pleases. He has already announced that all young men in Germany will receive military training.

Trainloads of cheering troops are leaving Rome to swell the ever-growing Italian army in East Africa.

RISK OF WAR IN EAST AFRICA

May, Since February, thousands of Italian troops have been moved to the frontier between Italian East Africa and Abyssinia. Mussolini blames Abyssinia. He claims that Abyssinian soldiers have fired across the border, and that Italian troops have been sent to stop them. The Abyssinians deny it. They say that the Italians are inventing reasons for invading their country. They have asked the League of Nations for protection.

A group of Abyssinian soldiers on the march—without shoes!

ITALY INVADES ABYSSINIA

Oct. 3, Italian East Africa Thousands of Italian troops crossed the border into Abyssinia at dawn this morning. The Italians have the most modern weapons, including at least 200 tanks. The Abyssinians are armed with simple rifles, and many have only spears and bows and arrows to fight with.

Social Security Act Signed Today

Aug. 14, Washington President Roosevelt today signed the Social Security Act into law. This legislation will provide a pension for the elderly. It will also supply some assistance to the handicapped, dependent children, and the unemployed.

The provisions of the new Social Security Act represent some of the reforms promised by Franklin D. Roosevelt's "New Deal" program.

NO GUNS FOR ITALY

Nov. 18, Geneva The League of Nations is at last trying to force Mussolini to end his invasion of Abyssinia. Fifty countries have agreed not to sell war weapons or supplies to Italy. However, the ban is likely to fail since oil is not included. So long as Italy can buy oil for its armed forces and industries, Mussolini will be able to continue the war against Abyssinia.

Hughes Sets New Speed Record

Sept. 15 Thirty-three-year-old industrialist, Hollywood motion-picture producer, and aviator Howard Hughes today flew a plane of his own design four times over a closed course at an average of 352 miles per hour. This feat sets a new world record for speed in aviation.

A man of many accomplishments, Hughes is becoming known as one of the world's richest men.

MAO'S LONG MARCH

Oct. 20, Shensi Province, China The Red Army has reached northern China. In this remote place it will be safe from attack by Chiang Kai-Shek's Nationalist forces. The Red Army has traveled over 5,590 miles in the year since it broke out of its base in the south. Only 30,000 soldiers remain of the 100,000 that set out. "The Long March," as Mao calls it, is the longest march in the history of war.

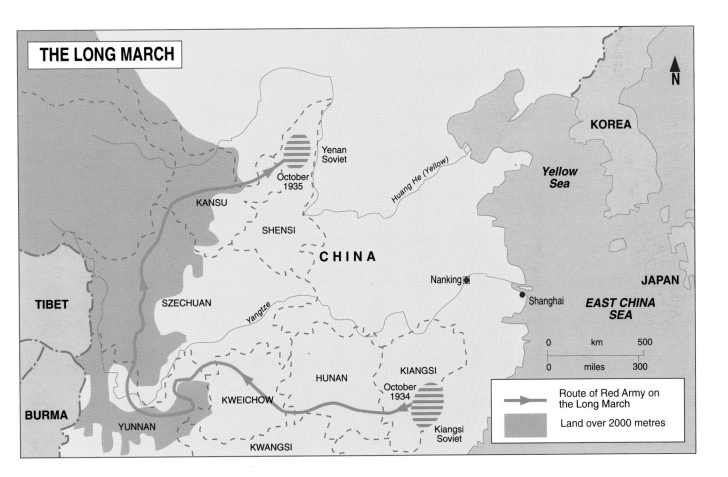

THE LONG MARCH

- Route of Red Army on the Long March
- Land over 2000 metres

NEWS IN BRIEF . . .

DUST DEVASTATES THE HEART OF AMERICA

April 15, Blinding dust storms have destroyed the rich farming country in America's heartland. The big choking dust clouds have ruined crops worth millions of dollars and driven thousands of people from their homes.

MAJOR IMPROVEMENT IN PASSENGER FLIGHTS

Dec. 21, New York Cross-country air travelers can look forward to more comfortable flights. American Airlines today introduced an improved passenger plane—the Douglas DC-3. This is a large plane with a 95-foot wing span, and it easily seats 21 passengers. Or 14 passengers can relax in its restful sleeping berths.

Powered by two big engines, the new plane flies at 160 miles per hour. It has the longest flight range of any commercial airplane in the world. American Airlines plans to use the Douglas DC-3 on coast-to-coast overnight flights.

NAZIS BAN JAZZ MUSIC

Oct., Berlin The Nazis have banned all jazz music composed by Jews and Negroes from German radio. The official announcement claims that such music is poor quality and that it will do young Germans no good to listen to it.

NEW ALTITUDE RECORD

Nov. 11, Two Americans have set a new altitude record for balloons. They reached a height of almost 74,000 feet.

MALCOLM CAMPBELL'S NEW WORLD RECORD

Sept. 3, Bonneville Salt Flats, Utah Sir Malcolm Campbell has broken the world land speed record for the **eighth** time! The English racer has taken his monster car *Bluebird* across the bed of this dried-up lake near Salt Lake City at 301 mph.

Sir Malcolm says that this is his last high speed drive on land. He now means to go for the world speed record on water!

GERSHWIN'S *PORGY AND BESS* OPENS

Sept. 30, Boston An all-black cast performs George Gershwin's opera *Porgy and Bess* which opens in Boston today. Critics predict it will become an American classic. The song "Summertime" is likely to become an all-time favorite.

1936

BRITAIN'S NEW KING

Jan. 20, London   King George V has died, aged 70. He reigned for 25 years and celebrated his Silver Jubilee only last year.

The king's eldest son Edward, Prince of Wales, now succeeds to the throne. He will take the title of King Edward VIII. The new king is unmarried. Until he marries and has children, the heir to the throne is his younger brother, the Duke of York.

NEW EGYPTIAN KING

April 28, Cairo, Egypt   Following the death of his father King Faud I, sixteen-year-old Prince Farouk tonight succeeds to the throne of Egypt. He now becomes King Farouk I.

ROOSEVELT WINS AGAIN

Nov. 3, Washington   The American people have elected Franklin D. Roosevelt to be our President for the second time. He won by the largest margin of votes in American history.

Most Americans are grateful to the President. His "New Deal" policy has given them jobs, and saved their homes, their farms, and their savings.

O'NEILL WINS NOBEL PRIZE FOR LITERATURE

Dec. 10, Stockholm, Sweden   New York-born playwright Eugene O'Neill has won the 1936 Nobel Prize for literature. O'Neill was a colorful adventurer in his early years. He has been a reporter, a sailor, and a homeless person. O'Neill also won a Pulitzer Prize for his 1920 play *Beyond the Horizon*. A more recent work is *Ah, Wilderness*.

CIVIL WAR IN SPAIN

SPANISH CIVIL WAR (July/August 1936)

Santander, Guernica, FRANCE, Bilbao, Vigo, Burgos *(Nationalist Government Headquarters)*, Salamanca, Madrid, CATALONIA, Barcelona, PORTUGAL, SPAIN, Minorca, Majorca, Lisbon, Ibiza, Seville, Granada, ATLANTIC OCEAN, Cadiz, Gibraltar *(British)*, Tangier, SPANISH MOROCCO

0 mi 150

Initial advance of Nationalists
Nationalist territory
Republican territory

July 31, Spain The Spanish army has rebelled against the government. General Franco, the army's leader, has accused the government of turning Spain into a Communist state. He has founded a new political party, the Nationalists, to oppose communism and has appealed to all Spaniards to join it.

Spaniards who side with the government call themselves "Republicans." They outnumber Franco's supporters, but Franco controls the army. In reply, the Republicans have formed an army of their own. Compared with Franco's forces, they are poorly trained and short of weapons. Fighting between the two sides is going on in many places. Spain is in the grip of civil war.

"VOLUNTEERS" FIGHT IN SPAIN

Dec. 31, Madrid There is no end in sight to the fighting in Spain. The war has spread. Italian and German troops and aircraft are serving with Franco's Nationalist forces. Russia is backing the Republicans with money, troops, and equipment. But the governments of these countries deny that they are involved in the war. They claim that all their men fighting in Spain are volunteers.

ITALY CONQUERS ABYSSINIA

May 9, Italian troops have occupied Addis Ababa, the capital of Abyssinia. The emperor and most of his family have escaped abroad. It is believed that he will make his home in Britain. The city of Rome has gone wild. Signor Benito Mussolini, speaking from a balcony to huge cheering crowds below, has proclaimed that Abyssinia belongs to Italy. "At last Italy has her empire," he said.

An Italian military governor will rule the new possession and the king of Italy will take the title "Emperor of Abyssinia."

German troops enter the Rhineland

March 6, French/German border Hitler's troops have occupied the Rhineland. After World War I, this strip of land between Germany and France was made neutral. No troops were to be stationed there. The area was meant to be a buffer between the two countries to keep them apart.

Other European powers have protested to Germany for taking over the Rhineland, but it is unlikely that they will try to force it to withdraw. They are frightened of Germany's growing strength, and are terrified of starting another war.

A street patrol in Barcelona, Spain. Civilians armed by the government use an old horse-drawn wagon for patrol duties.

NEWS IN BRIEF . . .

A NEW CAR FOR GERMANY

Feb. 26, Wolfsburg, Germany The Germans mean to become a nation on wheels — like the Americans! Herr Hitler has opened a new factory here, to produce a cheap, reliable car that every family will be able to afford. It is called "The People's Car." Its German name is *Volkswagen*.

RECORD ATLANTIC CROSSING

July, New Jersey The giant German airship *Hindenburg* has crossed the Atlantic in under two days. If the present tests continue to go well Germany will start a regular service across the Atlantic next year.

JESSE OWENS TRIUMPHS

Aug. 15, Berlin The XIth Olympic Games ended today. Germany and the U.S. have won most medals. The outstanding athlete of the Games is the black American runner Jesse Owens. He won four gold medals.

This triumph has enraged Germany's Nazi rulers. They claim that black people are inferior to whites. Yet, at the Berlin Games, a black athlete has shown he is the best in the world.

KING EDWARD VIII GIVES UP THRONE

Dec. 10, London King Edward VIII today gave up the throne of Great Britain to marry a twice-divorced American woman, Wallis Warfield Simpson. In a broadcast from Windsor Castle, the king told his subjects that he found it impossible "to carry the heavy burden of responsibility and to discharge my duties as king as I would wish to do without the help and support of the woman I love."

Political and religious leaders in Britain have tried to persuade King Edward to give up Mrs. Simpson. They said that people would never accept a divorced woman as his wife. However, Edward has refused to change his mind, preferring to abdicate.

Edward's younger brother Albert, the Duke of York, will reign in his place. When Albert is crowned, he will become George VI, King of England and Emperor of India.

1937

THE INTERNATIONAL BRIGADES

Feb. 20, Spain Volunteers from many countries are coming to Spain to take part in the war. Nearly all have joined the Republican side to fight General Franco. Many have had to come in secret. In some countries it is against the law to go to Spain to fight. The volunteers go into battle in units called the "International Brigades."

New Palestine Plan

July 7, London Because of the continuing conflict and violence between Arabs and Jews, the British propose to divide Palestine into three sectors. Two thirds will remain Arab. One third will become the Jewish sector. According to reports, neither Arab nor Jewish leaders are very pleased with this arrangement.

Arab landowners will be paid for the property they will be forced to give up. Also the three "holy cities" of Jerusalem, Bethlehem, and Nazareth will be permanently controlled by the British according to the new proposal.

Japan Bombs U.S. Ship

Dec. 1937, Washington The U.S. gunboat *Panay* was bombed and sunk by the Japanese on the Yangtze River in China. The United States has accepted an official apology from Japan. However, relations between the two countries remain tense.

THE BOMBING OF GUERNICA

April 30, Northern Spain Guernica has been destroyed. More than 100 German aircraft dropped tons of fire and high-explosive bombs on this defenseless small city. It was market day and the streets were crowded. The bombers came without warning. Over 2,000 men, women, and children were killed or injured.

The bombing of Guernica has aroused shock and anger throughout the world. Newspapers in Spain that support General Franco blame the other side. They claim that Republican troops deliberately destroyed Guernica before leaving it. Their story is a lie. From all reports and from the people who were there, it is certain that German bombers destroyed Guernica.

FRANCO IS WINNING THE WAR

Oct. 21, Northern Spain General Franco's forces are winning the civil war in Spain. Today they have captured the town of Gijon and 6,000 Republican prisoners. The Nationalists now control most of the country.

JAPANESE TAKE PEKING

July 28, Peking, China After three weeks of heavy fighting the Japanese have taken the city of Peking. More Japanese troops are pouring into China and are making for the port of Tientsin. They are likely to capture it in the next few days.

SHANGHAI FALLS TO THE JAPANESE

Nov. 9, Shanghai After three months of savage fighting, the Japanese have captured Shanghai. The loss of Shanghai, their greatest port, is a great blow to the Chinese.

The League of Nations has strongly condemned the Japanese attack on China, but the Japanese have ignored this. The Chinese have appealed for help to the League but no country is prepared to go to their aid. Once more, it seems the League is powerless to keep peace in the world.

Buildings blazing in Shanghai after a Japanese air bomb set the city alight.

Chamberlain becomes British Prime Minister

May 28, London Neville Chamberlain has become Prime Minister of Great Britain. He succeeds Stanley Baldwin, who has resigned.

Mr. Chamberlain was an excellent Minister of Health. He looked after Britain's finances well as Chancellor of the Exchequer. However, some people are worried that he knows so little about foreign affairs.

FDR Salutes Marchers in Inauguration Parade

Jan. 20, Washington President Franklin D. Roosevelt was sworn in for a second term today. This inauguration was the first not held on March 23. Under a cold, rainy sky, Roosevelt rode to the Capitol in an open limousine as cheering crowds lined his route.

In his address, Roosevelt expressed optimism for the nation's steady recovery from the Depression. However, on a somber note he said, "I see one-third of a nation ill-housed, ill-clad, ill-nourished."

Roosevelt is shown here with members of his family, Vice President Garner, officers of the armed forces, and others on the porch of the "Hermitage." This building is a replica of Andrew Jackson's home in Tennessee. Roosevelt is shown here formally responding to the respectful salutes of marchers in the official inauguration parade in Washington, D.C.

NEWS IN BRIEF . . .

GIANT AIRSHIP EXPLODES

May 6, Lakehurst Airfield, N.J. The giant airship *Hindenburg* fell to the earth in flames tonight, a few yards from the end of its journey across the Atlantic. Watchers on the ground saw a blue flame dart along the airship's back as it drew up to the mooring mast. Seconds later, the one and a half million cubic yards of hydrogen gas that kept the *Hindenburg* aloft caught fire. In a few moments, the airship had become a tangled heap of white-hot metal lying on the ground. It is believed that 34 people on board have died in the flames.

GREAT COMPOSER DIES

July 11, Hollywood, Calif. George Gershwin died in a Hollywood hospital today. He was only 38. Gershwin was born in New York. At 20 he was a well-known song-writer. He composed the famous *Rhapsody in Blue* and the music for a string of very successful shows like *Lady be Good*, *Funny Face*, and *Strike up the Band*. America has lost a genius.

JOE LOUIS: HEAVYWEIGHT CHAMPION

June 3, New York Joe Louis, from Detroit, is the new heavyweight champion of the world. He knocked out the former champion James J. Braddock in the eighth round of their fight. Joe Louis is 23 years old and is the first black boxer in 22 years to hold the title. His nickname is "The Brown Bomber."

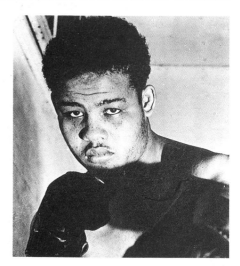

THE TERROR OF WAR

Oct., Paris A painting called *Guernica* has attracted enormous interest at the World Fair in Paris. The artist, Pablo Picasso, is a Spaniard. He painted the picture to protest the destruction of Guernica by German bombers earlier this year.

Picasso's painting, *Guernica.*

1938

HITLER THREATENS WAR

Sept. 27, Germany Prime Minister Neville Chamberlain has flown to meet Hitler for the second time in two weeks. Mr. Chamberlain hopes face-to-face talks will solve the latest crisis in Europe. Hitler demands that the parts of Czechoslovakia where Germans live be handed over to Germany. He threatens to take them by force if necessary.

Nazi propaganda poster designed to unite the German people behind Adolf Hitler — "One people, one nation, one leader."

British Prime Minister Neville Chamberlain with Adolf Hitler in Munich.

Churchill says, "Don't give in to Hitler"

Sept. 28, London Member of the British Parliament Mr. Winston Churchill continues to argue that Mr. Chamberlain is wrong to give in to Hitler's demands. He insists that Britain and France should declare that they will fight if the Czechs are attacked. Large crowds attended a meeting held in London to back Mr. Churchill's stand against Nazi Germany.

Air raid precautions in London: the entrance to a police station is protected by sandbags.

Neville Chamberlain on his return to England from Munich, Germany, with the crowd that greeted him at Heston Airport.

MUNICH MEETING ENDS CRISIS

Sept. 30, London Joyful crowds welcomed British Prime Minister Chamberlain back from Munich as he landed at Heston Airport this evening. He thanked the people for their greeting and waved a piece of paper signed by Herr Hitler and himself. It declared that Britain and Germany would never go to war again. "It is peace for our time," he said.

The crisis was ended at a meeting between the leaders of France, Italy, and Britain. They agreed that Germany should be allowed to take over the mainly German parts of Czechoslovakia. In return, Hitler has stated there is nothing else he wants from the Czechs, and will leave them in peace. The other leaders have accepted his promise.

There is relief in London but in Prague, the Czech capital, there is anger and dismay. The Czechs claim that Britain and France have betrayed them by giving in to Hitler. They were not even invited to the meeting in Munich that decided their fate.

GERMAN TROOPS INVADE AUSTRIA

March 14, Vienna, Austria German troops have crossed the border into Austria. Church bells rang and crowds cheered to welcome Adolf Hitler as he drove through the streets of the Austrian capital, Vienna, today.

The new Austrian Chancellor, Seyss Inquart, is a member of the Nazi party, and supports Adolf Hitler. He invited the Germans to invade Austria. German is the national language of Austria, and many Austrians would like their country to become part of Germany.

Hitler was born in Austria. Now that his native land is part of Germany he is ruler over 74 million people. Germany has become the most powerful country in Europe.

GERMANS ATTACK AUSTRIAN JEWS

March 18, Vienna The Germans have lost no time in attacking Jews in Austria. They have issued orders that prevent Jews from being lawyers, doctors, or teachers. Jewish shopkeepers and businessmen have been forced to put up notices that say "Jewish owned" outside their premises.

As part of their increasingly violent campaign against the Jews, the Nazis are smashing Jewish store windows and warning customers away with notices that say "Germans! Defend yourselves! Don't buy from Jews."

Danger of war over Czechoslovakia

May 20, Prague, Czechoslovakia A dangerous crisis here threatens to plunge Europe and perhaps the world into another war.

German troops now surround Czechoslovakia on three sides. Thousands of Germans live on the Czech side of the border. They claim that the Czech authorities treat them badly and persecute them for being German. Their leaders have appealed to Germany for protection.

If Germany does attack Czechoslovakia, it is hard to see how Britain and France could avoid being drawn into the conflict.

FRANCO CLAIMS VICTORY

April 15, Spain Units of General Franco's army have reached the coast of Spain at Vinaroz. This latest advance by the Nationalists has cut the Republican forces in two. General Franco claims that victory for his side is now certain.

Germans terrorize Jews

Nov. 11, Berlin Two nights ago, all over Germany, mobs attacked Jews. They burned down synagogues and beat up Jews in the streets. Thousands of Jewish shops were broken into and looted. So much shattered glass littered the streets that the Germans are calling the affair "Kristallnacht" — "the night of broken glass."

The German government blames it all on the Jews. It claims that the German people turned on them in anger when they heard the news that a Jew had murdered a German diplomat in Paris.

GERMANY ATTACKS CZECHOSLOVAKIA

N

DENMARK

USSR

Danzig

BRITAIN

London NETH.
Berlin

BELGIUM

GERMANY

POLAND

Rhine

Prague

CZECHOSLOVAKIA

Paris

Vienna

SWITZERLAND

AUSTRIA

HUNGARY

FRANCE

Danube

0   mi   300

German-speaking areas of Czechoslovakia

YUGOSLAVIA

ITALY

NEWS IN BRIEF . . .

SNOW WHITE AND THE SEVEN DWARFS

Jan., Hollywood Walt Disney's film *Snow White and the Seven Dwarfs* is a huge success. Audiences all over America are flocking to see it. Snow White is the first full-length cartoon film to appear on the screen.

ITALY KEEPS WORLD CUP

June 19, Paris The Italian soccer team has won the World Cup for the second time. They beat the Hungarians 4–2 in the final here in Paris.

Walt Disney, the creator of Mickey Mouse, has produced another cartoon success with the film *Snow White and the Seven Dwarfs*.

LABOR LAW SIGNED

June 25, Washington President Roosevelt today signed the Fair Labor Standards Act. It sets the minimum wage at 25 cents an hour for this year. It also calls for a maximum 44-hour work week.

CHILDREN GET USED TO THEIR GAS MASKS

Sept. 20, London The British government is providing a free gas mask for every citizen in the country. Children in school have been given practice in wearing their masks. It is feared that bombs containing poison gas would be dropped on Britain if war were to come.

ORSON WELLES ON RADIO SCARES AMERICANS

Oct. 30, New York Last night listeners to Welles's radio show heard his version of a science fiction story about a Martian invasion of Earth. Many people believed that men from Mars really were landing in New Jersey. Terrified listeners made frantic phone calls to the police.

KATE SMITH SINGS ''GOD BLESS AMERICA''

Nov. 12, New York On her radio show last night ''First Lady of Radio'' Kate Smith made an instant hit with the song ''God Bless America.'' Written by Irving Berlin in 1918, it was never sung publicly until Miss Smith sang it here in honor of Armistice Day.

1939

WORLD IN CRISIS

HITLER THREATENS THE CZECHS

March 13, Berlin Hitler has sent a list of demands to the Czech government which they will find impossible to meet. Meanwhile, the Nazi newspapers and radio have begun a campaign of hate against the Czech people.

Hitler returned to Berlin last night and received the salutes and cheers from nearly 1,000,000 people following the successful invasion of Czechoslovakia.

GERMANY INVADES CZECHOSLOVAKIA

March 15, Prague German troops have moved into Czechoslovakia. Hitler explains the invasion by claiming that the Czechs have ignored the demands he made on them a few days ago.

Czechs weep as Germans drive through Prague

March 16, Prague Czechs showed anger and bitterness as invading German troops drove through their capital, Prague, today. Some stood silent, some hissed and booed, some shook their fists. Many wept to see their country occupied by a hated enemy. Hitler has boasted publicly, "Czechoslovakia has ceased to exist."

Forced to salute in the Nazi manner, Czechs weep as German soldiers march through the streets of their capital, Prague.

CZECH INVASION SHOCKS THE WORLD

March 17, Hitler's annexation of Czechoslovakia has stunned the world. Six months after promising at Munich to leave Czechoslovakia in peace, he has seized the country and made it part of Germany. In London, Prime Minister Chamberlain has spoken of his "shock" at Hitler's action. Both the French and British governments are sending formal notes to Berlin protesting at the German invasion of Czechoslovakia.

World's Fair Opens

April 30, New York The huge Trylon and Perisphere (below) symbolize the New York World's Fair formally opened today by President Roosevelt. The official theme of the Fair is progress and peace. However, thoughts of war were in many minds here today, and Germany was not among the 60 exhibitor nations.

POLAND ATTACKED

N

Free City of Danzig

EAST PRUSSIA

USSR

Warsaw

POLAND

GERMANY

→ German and Russian attacks

Polish Corridor
- a narrow strip of land which is Poland's route or "corridor" to the sea

0   mi   150

HITLER THREATENS POLAND

March 31, Berlin The port of Danzig was once part of Germany but after World War I the League of Nations made it a free city. Danzig is Poland's only outlet to the sea. The Poles insist that it must remain independent. Hitler demands that Danzig should be returned to Germany and threatens to take it by force, if necessary. Britain and France have promised to go to Poland's aid if she is attacked by Germany. The three countries will sign a formal treaty.

Russia and Germany sign friendship agreement

Aug. 23, Moscow Russia and Germany have signed an agreement not to go to war with each other. Britain and France are dismayed by the news. They hoped to persuade Russia to join them in a pact to protect Poland against an attack by Germany. This surprise agreement means that Hitler can invade Poland without fear of war with Russia.

GERMANY INVADES POLAND

Sept. 1, Poland Early this morning, German troops tore down barriers along the Polish border and crossed into Poland. They are now advancing rapidly everywhere.

RUSSIA ATTACKS POLAND

Sept. 17, Poland Russian troops have invaded Poland. Their aim is to occupy as much of the land as possible before the Germans reach it. The Polish army is trapped and cannot hold out much longer.

BRITAIN AND FRANCE DECLARE WAR ON GERMANY

Sept. 3, London Britain and France are at war with Germany. Hitler has not replied to their demand to withdraw his troops from Poland, so war has been declared. Prime Minister Chamberlain gave the news to the British people in a radio broadcast at 11:15 this morning.

BRITISH TROOPS LAND IN FRANCE

Sept. 27, France 150,000 British troops with their equipment and vehicles have landed in France. They are the first part of a larger force that is to follow. The British units will take up positions beside their French allies facing the Germans. Very little fighting has taken place so far.

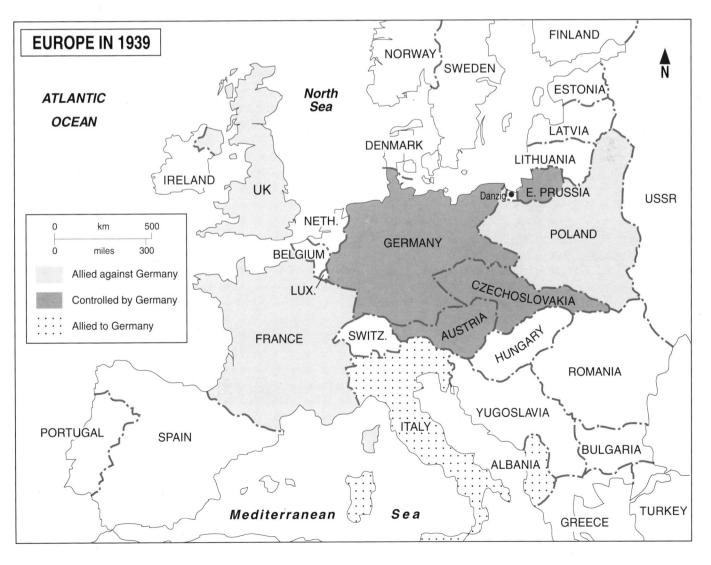

EUROPE IN 1939

Scale:
0 — 500 km
0 — 300 miles

Allied against Germany
Controlled by Germany
Allied to Germany

FALL OF MADRID ENDS SPANISH CIVIL WAR

March 28, Madrid The Republicans in Madrid have surrendered. General Franco is victorious. The civil war in Spain is over. But Franco faces huge problems. Spain is deeply in debt. Many towns and cities are in ruins and thousands of factories destroyed. Hundreds of thousands of farm animals have died. Trade and industry are at a standstill after the long bloody conflict.

Swing's the Thing

Aug. 5, New York An enthusiastic couple "jitterbugs" in the Swing Casino at the World's Fair. Dancing to the wildly popular form of jazz called swing entertains hundreds of young people daily at the Fair. "Swing fever" continues to be a colorful part of the current American scene at the largest world's fair in history. Bandleader Benny Goodman is known as the "King of Swing."

Marian Anderson Silenced

Feb. 27, Washington The Daughters of the American Revolution, a woman's organization, has refused to allow famous Negro contralto Marian Anderson to sing at Constitution Hall. The D.A.R. owns this Washington auditorium.

Wizard of Oz Opens

Aug. 18, Hollywood The film version of Frank Baum's classic children's book *The Wonderful Wizard of Oz* had its premiere tonight. The story of Dorothy, who is blown by a tornado from her home in Kansas to the magical land of Oz, cost its producers $3 million. This entertaining fantasy stars Judy Garland as Dorothy, Bert Lahr as the Cowardly Lion, Ray Bolger as the Scarecrow, and Jack Haley as the Tin Man.

British children moved to safety

Sept. 2, London Over 1½ million British children are being evacuated from their homes in the cities to stay with families in the country. The government fears that London and other civilian centers will be bombed if war comes. Plans were made earlier to take the city children to safer places if war seemed certain.

British victory at the battle of the Plate River

Dec. 17, Montevideo, Uruguay The German pocket battleship *Graf Spee* has sunk. She was blown up by her own crew. British warships were lying in wait as the *Graf Spee* left Montevideo harbor. There was no way of escape, so the German crew sent her to the bottom. For weeks the British navy has been searching the seas for the *Graf Spee*. This victory will do much to lift British spirits.

The *Graf Spee* sinks in the estuary of the Plate River. Following the recent losses of the aircraft carrier *Courageous* and the battleship *Royal Oak* this victory will do much to raise British spirits.

NEWS IN BRIEF . . .

NEW WONDER FABRIC "NYLON" HITS THE SHOPS

Feb. 21, New York Women's stockings made of nylon have gone on sale for the first time. They cost $1.15 a pair. Nylon looks and feels like silk but is much cheaper, washes more easily, and lasts longer. Other garments made of nylon are on the way. Women's underwear and men's shirts will follow soon.

TELEVISION ARRIVES

April 30, New York America's first regular television service made its first broadcast today! Television cameras filmed President Roosevelt as he opened the New York's World's Fair.

FIRST TRANSATLANTIC PASSENGER FLIGHT

July 3, Long Island Pan American Airways will soon begin its regular passenger flights to England. In a test flight today the Boeing seaplane will fly from Long Island to Newfoundland, then to Ireland, and finally end its journey in Southampton Water in England.

Pan American Airways is using the Boeing 314 flying boat *Yankee Clipper* for its new transatlantic passenger flights.

PEOPLE OF THE THIRTIES

Neville Chamberlain 1869–1940

British Prime Minister Chamberlain entered the British Parliament in 1918 as a member of the Tory, or Conservative, party. He became Prime Minister in 1937. Chamberlain knew little about foreign affairs and Hitler was able to fool him completely over the Czech crisis (see page 38). He took Britain into the war in 1939, but resigned in 1940. He died of cancer six months later.

Marie Curie, Polish/French scientist 1867–1934

Marie Curie was Polish but moved to France to study science. There she married a scientist, Pierre Curie. Together they studied the strange rays given off by the metal uranium. After Pierre died Marie continued their work. In 1911 she received a Nobel Prize for discoveries in radioactivity which are vital to the cure for cancer. She died of a blood disorder caused by the radioactivity that made her famous. (See page 23.)

Walt Disney, American filmmaker 1901–1966

Walt Disney has probably done more to entertain people than anyone who has ever lived. His most famous creation was Mickey Mouse. Mickey first appeared in 1928, and in the thirties was joined by Minnie Mouse, Donald Duck, Goofy, Pluto, and a cast of other characters that are known and loved around the world. Disney went on to produce full-length cartoons and adventure films. (See page 36.)

Francisco Franco 1892–1975

Spanish dictator. Franco organized the revolt against the government that set off the Spanish civil war. He ended the war as head of state in Spain. He ruled Spain as a dictator from 1937 until his death in 1975. (See page 40.)

Mahatma Gandhi 1869–1948

Indian independence leader. Gandhi trained as a lawyer. After World War I he became leader of the movement to end British rule in India. He persuaded his followers to defy British laws, but never to use violence. Millions followed his example of peaceful disobedience. India won independence in 1948, but a religious fanatic murdered Gandhi a few months later. (See page 16.)

George Gershwin, American composer 1898–1937

George Gershwin's parents were Russian Jews who had come to live in New York City. Young George loved music but was too poor to pay for lessons, so he taught himself. His song "Swanee" made him famous before he was twenty years old. George Gershwin wrote the music for many successful stage shows and movies. (See page 32.)

Adolf Hitler 1889–1945

Hitler was born in Austria, but moved to Germany. In 1933 he became dictator of Germany. He seized Austria and Czechoslovakia and, in 1939, invaded Poland. World War II followed. Hitler won many victories at first, but was finally defeated by the combined forces of Russia, America, and Britain. He killed himself in 1945, the night before the Russians entered Berlin.

Franklin D. Roosevelt 1882–1945

President of the United States. Roosevelt was crippled by polio and could not stand or walk without help. In spite of this, he was elected President. In the 1930s, his New Deal policy rescued America from the world economic depression. He led the United States into World War II in 1941, against Germany and Japan. In 1944 he became President for a record fourth time, but died in April 1945 just before victory.

Pablo Picasso, Spanish artist 1881–1973

Pablo Picasso was a Spaniard, but moved to Paris in 1904. He spent the rest of his life in France where he produced a huge variety of paintings, drawings, prints, and sculptures. His work had a powerful influence on other artists of his time. The painting *Guernica* (see page 32) was Picasso's protest at the cruelty and horror of the civil war in Spain.

Benito Mussolini 1883–1945

Italian dictator Mussolini was a teacher and then a journalist. He entered politics and became leader of the Fascist party. In 1922 he became Prime Minister of Italy. He got rid of those who opposed him and by 1929 had become an all-powerful dictator. In 1935 he seized the country of Abyssinia in Africa. He became Hitler's ally in World War II, but was defeated in 1943. He was shot by Italian freedom fighters in 1945.

Joseph Stalin 1879–1953

Communist dictator. Stalin was a leader of the revolution of 1917 in Russia, which put the Communists in power in that country. He got rid of everyone who stood in his way, and became sole dictator. Russia was then very backward. Stalin brought it up to date. Those who opposed the changes "disappeared." Millions of people died on his orders. In World War II, Stalin led Russia to victory over Nazi Germany.

Mao Tse-Tung 1893–1976

First leader of Communist China. In 1921 the Chinese Communist party was founded. Mao was one of those who helped establish it. In 1934–35 he led the Long March of the Communist army through all opposition to a safe place in northern China. After World War II, he defeated the Nationalists under Chiang Kai-Shek, and made China into a Communist state. (See page 25.)

American Firsts

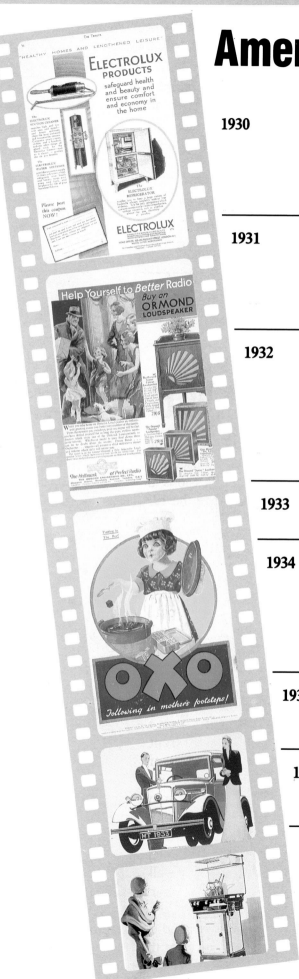

1930

Television reception in the home demonstrated, in New York City.

Thomas A. Edison installs an experimental electric passenger train on tracks between Hoboken and Montclair, New Jersey.

1931

Nonstop flight across the Pacific Ocean completed by American pilots Hugh Herndon and Clyde Pangborn.

An American woman, Jane Addams, wins the Nobel Peace Prize.

1932

Development of a yellow fever vaccine to immunize human beings announced.

Edwin H. Land invents Polaroid glass.

H.O.W. Caraway is first woman to be elected to the Senate.

Lou Gehrig becomes the first baseball player to hit four home runs in a row in a single game.

1933

In Camden, New Jersey, the first drive-in movie theater opens.

1934

In Fort Worth, Texas, the first washing machines installed for public use.

Dr. Wallace H. Carothers of DuPont laboratories produces nylon.

In San Francisco, first U.S. general strike takes place.

1935

First parking meters installed, in Oklahoma City.

First use of a lie detector allowed in court, in Portage, Wisconsin.

1936

In Cooperstown, New York, the Baseball Hall of Fame opened.

First all-glass building erected, in Toledo, Ohio.

1937

In Chicago, first blood bank opens.

The first radio program broadcasts coast-to-coast.

In Connecticut, country's first permanent automobile license plates issued.

1938	The first radar-equipped passenger ship goes into operation.
	The self-propelled combine goes into use on American farms, to replace the tractor-driven combine.
	A woman, Pearl S. Buck, wins the Nobel Prize for literature.
1939	First successful helicopter built, in Stratford, Connecticut.
	An air-conditioned car is shown to public in Chicago, Illinois.

New words and expressions

The English language is always changing. New words are added to it, and old words are used in new ways. Here are a few of the words and expressions that first appeared or first came into popular use in the 1930s:

accident-prone	offbeat
air-condition	okeydoke
bed-and-breakfast	picture tube
big band	piece of cake
candid camera	pig latin
caseload	pinball machine
double agent	playpen
double take	power steering
expressway	private eye
folding money	prowl car
glove compartment	rat race
groovy	rent control
housing project	senior citizen
Ivy League	swing shift
jalopy	snowsuit
jam session	supermarket
jukebox	tea bag
lindy hop	telephone number
mercy killing	walkathon
newscaster	worrywart

How many of these words and expressions do we still use today? Do you know what they all mean?

Glossary

Abyssinia: a country in northeast Africa now called Ethiopia.

Chancellor: head of the government in Germany and Austria.

communism: a political theory. Communists believe that all property and industry in a country should belong to the state.

concentration camps: During the Boer War 1899–1902 the British set up internment camps to hold the families of Boer commando fighters. These camps became known as "concentration camps." The Nazis borrowed this term for the camps they built to imprison enemies of the state.

dictator: a ruler who has total power in his own country, for example, Hitler, Stalin, and Mussolini.

diplomat: an official sent abroad to represent his or her country to another government.

gulag: a prison camp in Soviet Russia.

kulak: a Russian peasant who owned land.

League of Nations: the international organization set up after World War I to keep peace between nations and solve world problems by discussion.

Mahatma: an Indian title meaning "great and wise" for example, Mahatma Gandhi.

Nationalists: In Spain, the party, led by General Franco, that supported strong central government by a dictator.

Nazi: the short form in German of "The National Socialist German Workers' Party"

New Deal: President Roosevelt's program, in 1933, for rebuilding the American economy after the Depression. He called it a "New Deal" for America.

Nobel Prize: given to people who have done something very important for world peace, or in science or literature.

Prime Minister: the head of some governments.

Reichstag: the German parliament and the building it met in.

republic: a country in which the head of state (usually a president) is chosen by vote.

Republicans: (also known as the Popular Front) In Spain the party of the Socialists, trade unions, and those who stood for a government elected by the votes of the people.

synagogue: a building in which Jews hold religious services.

Versailles Treaty: the treaty of 1919, named after the palace near Paris where it was signed, that ended World War I.

Further Reading

Allen, Eleanor. *Wartime Children, Nineteen Thirty-Nine to Nineteen Forty-Five.* Dufour Editions, 1978

Bradley, Catherine. *Hitler and the Third Reich.* Watts, 1990

Cairns, Trevor. *Twentieth Century.* Lerner, 1984

Carey, Helen and Greenberg, Judith. *How to Read a Newspaper.* Watts, 1983

——How to Use Primary Sources. Watts, 1983

Faber, Doris and Harold. *Mahatma Gandhi.* Messner, 1986

Greenblatt, Miriam. *Franklin D. Roosevelt: 32nd President of the United States.* Garrett Ed., 1988

Marrin, Albert. *Stalin: Man of Steel.* Viking Penguin, 1988

Shirer, William L. *Rise and Fall of Adolf Hitler.* Random House, 1984

Townson, W.D., et al. *Picture History of the World.* Putnam, 1986

Index